THE
LITTLE
BREAKFAST
BOOK

Jennie Reekie

PIATKUS

ACKNOWLEDGEMENTS

The author and publishers would like to acknowledge the help of the following:

The Bircher-Benner Clinic
Frank Cooper Ltd
The Kellogg Company of Great Britain
The Wellcome Institute

First published in 1987 by
Judy Piatkus (Publishers) Limited,
5 Windmill Street, London W1P 1HF

British Library Cataloguing in Publication Data
Reekie, Jennie
    The little breakfast book.
    1. Breakfasts
    I. Title
    394.1′5   TX733

    ISBN 0-86188-655-8

Drawings by Trevor Newton
Designed by Sue Ryall
Cover illustration by Joanna Isles

Phototypeset in Linotron Plantin by
Phoenix Photosetting, Chatham
Printed and bound in Great Britain at
The Bath Press, Avon

CONTENTS

'If you would eat well in England,
you must eat breakfast three times a day.'

W. Somerset Maugham (1874-1965)

THE HISTORY OF BRITISH BREAKFASTS

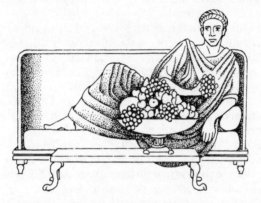

The first recorded breakfasters in Britain were the Romans. They generally ate a light breakfast at sunrise called the *ientaculum*, which consisted of bread and fresh fruit. These rather modest breakfast habits were not, however, practised by Clodium Albinus, one of the last Roman ministers in Britain, who is reputed to have once consumed '500 figs, 100 peaches, 10 melons, 20lb grapes, 100 figpeckers and 400 oysters' for his first meal of the day!

After the departure of the Romans, the Anglo-Saxons continued to eat a simple breakfast at dawn, though fruit no longer constituted a part of it. In the Middle Ages the country people would start their day with curd cheese, broth or gruel and bread, accompanied by rather watery ale. The richer elements of society, on the other hand, ate boiled beef, mutton and pickled or salted herrings, also washed down with ale – doubtless of a stronger variety – and wine.

This pattern continued for several hundred years. Writing in her diary on the 10th May 1451, Elizabeth Woodville, wife of Edward IV, wrote: 'Breakfasted. The buttock of beef rather too much boiled, and the ale a little the stalest.'

Another writer in the same century breakfasted with her husband on 'two loaves of bread, a quart of beer, a quart of wine, two pieces of salt fish, six baconed herrings, four white herrings.' And in the 16th century, Queen Elizabeth I and her ladies were renowned for feasting on large quantities of beef and beer, occasionally supplemented by cheese.

By the early part of the 18th century, changes had begun to occur in the breakfasts served in the big houses. This was largely brought about by the availability of tea, coffee and chocolate, all of which quickly gained popularity with the gentry as excellent breakfast beverages. Their high price, however, meant that the poor continued to drink ale for a further 100 years.

In the country, the gentlemen would get up at around 7 a.m. and have a light breakfast before going shooting or following other country pursuits. The ladies would rise a couple of hours later and take a light breakfast of tea, coffee or chocolate with rusks or cake. Sherry and biscuits were served at about 11 a.m., and dinner at around 2 p.m. By the middle of the century, dinner was not served until nearer 4 p.m.

In town the gentry got off to an even later start. Ladies and gentlemen would breakfast on tea or chocolate and bread and butter between 10-11 o'clock. An hour later the gentlemen would leave for one of the coffee houses, returning home for dinner in the middle of the afternoon.

Gradually things began to change further down the social scale. The middle classes, as well as the working classes, began to work further away from their homes. They were unable to return at mid-day for a substantial lunch and so the importance of breakfast increased. Thus, by the middle of the 19th century, it was common to have a meal of porridge and bacon and eggs, mutton chops or potted meat or fish before leaving home. The era of the Great British Breakfast had begun.

THE GREAT BRITISH BREAKFAST

It is often thought that the zenith of The Great British Breakfast was the Victorian era, but in fact it reached its pinnacle during the glitter of the Edwardian age. Those were the days when, especially in large country houses, it was not unusual to have on offer at any one time fried, poached, scrambled and boiled eggs, fish cakes, a choice of devilled pheasant, roast quail, duck, partridge or ptarmigan, plus cold potted game and fish, whole hams, galantines, brawns, game pies and bowls of fresh fruit! As well as this, there was always porridge, toast, freshly made warm scones, jam, marmalade, tea and coffee.

The Victorians had certainly started the fashion. Mrs Beeton, who contributed to her husband's magazine in 1859–60, advised that for 'the comfortable meal called breakfast' one should serve 'cold joints, collared or potted meats, cold game, veal and ham pies, broiled fish, mutton chops and rump

4

steaks, kidney, sausages, bacon and poached eggs, muffins, toast, marmalade, butter, etcetera, etcetera.'

It became the fashion towards the end of the 19th century to dispense with the servants at breakfast time. They would prepare the table and leave the food on the sideboard to keep hot in chafing dishes. This method of self-service did not appeal to everyone, however. As Henry James observed in 1877, 'accordingly throughout the length and breadth of England, everyone who has the slightest pretension to standing high enough to feel the way the social breeze is blowing conforms'. He complained that it involved 'a vast amount of leaning and stretching, of waiting and perambulating.'

Breakfasts were leisurely meals which could, and indeed frequently did, last for hours. Sir Harold Nicolson (1886–1968), Vita Sackville-West's husband, described breakfast as follows: 'Edwardian breakfasts were in no sense a hurried proceeding. The porridge was disposed of negligently, people walking about and watching the rain descend upon the Italian garden. Then would come whiting and omelette and devilled kidneys and little fishy messes in shells. And then tongue and ham and a slice of ptarmigan. And scones and honey and marmalade. And then a little melon and a nectarine or two, and just one or two of those delicious raspberries!'

After the First World War there were fewer servants and fewer dishes ranged on the sideboard. But breakfast was still no mean affair, with cold ham and potted meats or a game pie still featuring, especially in the larger households. There was no longer a plethora of other hot dishes, however; merely a choice of one or two in addition to the standard bacon, eggs and sausages, mushrooms and smoked fish.

In a revised edition of Mrs Beeton's *Household Management*, published after the War when the good lady herself had been dead for nearly 50 years, the new editors wrote that 'eggs and bacon were too often the sheet-anchor of the English cook' and that there were 'over 200 ways of dressing eggs, to say nothing of grilled chops, steaks, cutlets, kidneys, fish and mushrooms, anchovy and sardine toast.' They prefaced this with their views on this first meal of the day: 'The moral and physical welfare of mankind depends largely on its breakfast, yet many of those upon whom the responsibility of providing it rests do not realise how far-reaching may be the effect of a good or bad meal. A being well fed and warmed is naturally on better terms with himself and his surroundings than one whose mind and body are being taxed by the discomfort and annoyance of badly cooked or insufficient food.'

One shudders to think of the dismay they must have felt if they were still alive during the Second World War. Then they would have felt themselves lucky if they had been able to obtain even some powdered egg! The First World War may have reduced the glory of the Great British Breakfast, but the Second annihilated it. The days of groaning sideboards were gone forever and breakfast was forced to become a simpler—and healthier—affair.

BEHIND THE GREEN BAIZE DOOR

By the time the Victorian and Edwardian family sat down to their breakfast at around 9 a.m., behind the green baize door some of the servants would have been working for several hours. The kitchenmaid would have risen at between 5 and 6 a.m., first blacking and polishing the stove and lighting it ready for Cook to start her work. Cook, being a more senior servant, would get up an hour later – and in some households she would be wakened by the kitchenmaid and brought a cup of tea in bed.

This description of the start of one young Victorian kitchenmaid's day is not something we would relish today!

'Get up at 5.30 a.m., blacklead a six foot cooking range, light the fire, scrub the kitchen tables and floor, then call the Cook and upper servants at 7 o'clock (with tea). It was a large house with a basement kitchen and scullery. I was given a thick taper to light my way down the back stairs, and told not to put on my shoes, so as not to disturb anyone. I shall never forget the horror of that first morning, the crunch under my stockinged feet when I opened the kitchen door to find the floor and all round the fireplace thick with huge black beetles.'

Breakfast for the staff (and the nursery if there were children in the household) took place at 8 a.m. and preparing this would be Cook's first job of the day. In larger households, with more than one kitchenmaid, the senior kitchenmaid might prepare staff breakfast, giving Cook more time for the family's meal. The staff breakfast was a fairly simple affair. Few servants went hungry, but what they were given was wholly dependent on the generosity of the mistress of the house and the cook. In some places their food simply consisted of slices of cold roast meat left from the night before. In others, bacon or eggs or sausages were served. It was unusual for the staff to have eggs and bacon together, other than as a treat on Sundays.

The cold dishes for the dining room would be taken in and set out on the sideboard in advance. Then Cook would have the task of attempting to have all the hot dishes ready together so that they could be dished up into the silver entreé dishes and put to keep warm on their spirit stoves on the sideboard. As breakfast was consumed 'upstairs', the planning for lunch and the rest of the day's meals took place 'downstairs' in the kitchen.

While breakfast, and indeed all the other meals, were quite lavish affairs, especially if the family had guests staying, the mistress of the house would expect Cook to practise thrift in the kitchen. Thus many of the traditional breakfast dishes, such as potted meats, kedgeree, fish cakes, etc., were an excellent way of discreetly making use of leftover fish, game, cold meats, and even boiled eggs from the previous day's breakfast.

POTTED PHEASANT

The practice of potting meat and fish was popular for hundreds of years. Once the cooked meat had been 'potted' it was covered with clarified butter to form a seal. Provided this was not broken, the meat would keep in the larder for up to two months.

5 oz (125 g) cooked pheasant
2 oz (50 g) softened butter
½ teaspoon made English mustard
1 teaspoon Worcestershire sauce
a good pinch dried thyme
meat juices (see method)
salt and freshly milled black pepper
clarified butter

Either mince the meat finely by hand or in a food processor. Turn into a basin and beat in the softened butter, then the mustard, Worcestershire sauce and thyme.

The addition of meat juices is not essential, but if you have any (do not use a thickened gravy though), beat them in, together with up to about 3 tablespoons of any fat left after cooking the bird.

Season to taste with salt and pepper, then pack into a pot. Seal the top with clarified butter. If sealed in this way, the meat will keep for two months, but once the seal has been broken it should be eaten within two days.

Serves 6

KEDGEREE

Kedgeree has been appearing on British breakfast tables for 200 years. Brought back from India in the 18th century by employees of the East India Company, the word is a derivation of the Hindi *khicheri* meaning hotchpotch. It originally consisted of rice, onion, red lentils, curry spices, fresh limes, butterfat and fish, but it has now become rather more mundane and is frequently just a mixture of rice, smoked haddock, eggs, butter and parsley. To the cognoscente, kedgeree should contain a hint of curry; the amount can be varied according to personal taste.

1 lb (450 g) smoked haddock fillet
salt
*6 oz (175 g) long grain rice (you can use brown if you
    prefer)*
1 oz (25 g) butter
1 medium-sized onion, peeled and finely chopped
2–3 teaspoons garam masala (according to taste)
2 tablespoons chopped parsley
1 tablespoon lemon juice
2 hard-boiled eggs, shelled and chopped
¼ pint (150 ml) single cream
freshly milled black pepper

Put the haddock into a pan, cover with cold water, bring to the boil, then remove from the heat and leave to stand for 10 minutes. Lift the fish out of the pan, peel off the skin and flake the flesh. Pour the liquor from cooking the fish into a pan. Add extra water, then taste and add extra salt if necessary. Add the rice and cook, following the instructions on the packet, until it is tender. Drain well.

Melt the butter in a pan, gently fry the onion with the garam masala for 5 minutes. Add the rice and mix well. Then add the smoked haddock, half the parsley, the lemon juice and chopped eggs and mix well. Cook for about 5 minutes, stirring frequently until piping hot, then stir in the cream and cook for a further minute. Taste and adjust the seasoning. Turn into a heated serving dish and sprinkle with the remaining parsley.

Serves 4

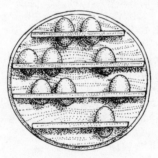

'No business before breakfast, Glum!'
says the King.
'Breakfast first, business next'.

Valoroso, William Thackery (1811-63)

DEVILLED KIDNEYS

Devilling, or giving dishes a hot, sharp flavour, was extremely fashionable throughout the 19th century. It was frequently used as a means of disguising the previous day's meat, game or poultry.

In the opinion of Dr Kitchiner, whose *Cook's Oracle* was published in 1817, devilling is also a hangover cure. His introduction to Devil Sauces runs as follows: 'Every man must have experienced that when he has got deep into his third bottle . . . his stomach is seized with a certain craving which seems to demand a stimulant. The provocatives used on such an occasion an ungrateful world has combined to term devil's.'

For more hangover cures, see page 58.

Devilled kidneys make an excellent and popular brunch dish today.

12 oz (350 g) lamb's kidneys
1½ oz (45 g) flour
2 oz (50 g) butter
1 medium-sized onion, peeled and chopped
¼ pint (150 ml) beef stock
2 teaspoons made English mustard
2 teaspoons Worcestershire sauce
3 anchovy fillets, finely chopped
salt (see method)
freshly milled black pepper

To garnish
1 tablespoon chopped parsley

Halve the kidneys, remove the cores and cut into ½ inch (1.25 cm) pieces. Toss in the flour. Melt the butter in a pan, add the onion and fry gently for 3–4 minutes. Increase the heat slightly, add the kidneys, and cook for a further 5 minutes, stirring frequently. Pour in the beef stock, blended with the mustard and Worcestershire sauce, and bring to the boil, stirring all the time. Reduce the heat, stir in the anchovies and simmer gently for a further 3–4 minutes. Taste and adjust the seasoning (adding salt if necessary).

Turn into a serving dish and sprinkle with the chopped parsley. Serve with hot toast or croûtons of fried bread.

Serves 4

The word breakfast is thought to have derived from the Middle English word *brekfast*, which in turn was a derivation of *breken*, meaning to break, and *fast*. And breakfast is just that – the breaking of the overnight fast.

REGIONAL SPECIALITIES

In addition to the classic breakfast dishes, there are also a number of regional specialities throughout the British Isles. In the North of England, sliced and fried black pudding was always considered to be an essential part of any recent breakfast. The Scots frequently add a slice of sweet suet pudding called clootie dumpling to a platter of bacon and egg. In Cornwall (and in the North of England and Ireland), cod's roe, which has first been boiled or poached and allowed to cool, is sliced and fried in bacon fat and served with rashers of crisply fried bacon. Laver bread (pounded and sieved seaweed found on the Pembrokeshire and other Welsh and Irish coasts) is fried in bacon fat and served with bacon and fried bread or toast in many parts of Wales. In Ireland, freshly baked soda bread is preferred to toast, while in Jersey, with its French influence, they prepare a dish which is not dissimilar to Cassoulet.

ARBROATH SMOKIES

The habit of eating smokies for breakfast may have died in England, but it is still very much alive and well in their native Scotland. A relation to the Finnan Haddie, the difference between them is that the smokie is hot smoked and the haddie is cold smoked.

Smokies were taken to Arbroath at the beginning of the 19th century by a group of fishermen from Auchmithie who settled there. It had long been a custom with them to hang their fish in the chimneys or lums of their cottages, and the canny people of Arbroath quickly realised the potential of this means of preserving the haddock catch. They improved slightly on the original method to make it more commercial by sinking halved whisky barrels into the ground, filling them with oak and silver birch chips and smoking the fish over these.

Smokies and haddies are still made in the same way today and as you enter Arbroath you are immediately assailed by the smell of smoking fish. Not possibly everyone's idea of an ambrosial smell, it is nevertheless interesting to see the fish being smoked. Every cottager is delighted to show you.

You can eat smokies cold, and they make marvellous pâtés and mousses. But for breakfast, they are traditionally dotted with butter, lightly grilled and served hot.

JERSEY BEAN JAR

In Jersey French or Patois this recipe is known as *Un Piot et des Pais au Fou*. In the days before everyone had an oven in their own home, women would take their crocks of beans down to the baker and he would cook them overnight in the oven as it cooled.

You should use as wide a mixture of beans for this as you possibly can: ideally a mixture of small and large white haricot beans, small brown beans, red kidney beans and butter beans.

1 lb (450 g) mixed beans (see above)
salt and freshly milled black pepper
1 teaspoon dried mixed herbs
1 lb (450 g) belly of pork
8 oz (225 g) bacon pieces or streaky bacon
1 pig's trotter

Soak the beans in cold water for between 12-24 hours. Drain well. Put into a pan and cover with 2 pints (1.2 litres) fresh cold water. Season with salt and pepper and add the herbs. Bring to the boil and simmer gently for 3 minutes. Tip into a casserole or crock.

Roughly chop the pork belly and bacon and split the pig's trotter. Bury the meat in the beans, then cover the pot with a lid. Put into a low oven, 250°F/120°C/Gas Mark ½, and leave to cook overnight. Taste and adjust the seasoning before serving.

Serves 4–6

CHANGING BREAKFAST HABITS

Rationing and changing lifestyles forced the British breakfast into a decline. At the end of the 1960s over half the population were still eating a cooked breakfast. It took a more limited form than before, consisting usually of a boiled egg, or egg, bacon and sausages, or kippers, those stalwarts of the British breakfast table. But around this time a number of factors combined to make it fall further out of favour.

The American ready-prepared breakfast cereals had established themselves before the War. Now they became an accepted part of everyday breakfast. Porridge, the traditional British cereal, developed as a dish only to be consumed in the winter months to 'keep out the cold', as the advertisements for instant porridge informed the population. People generally started to become more weight-conscious and to eat rather smaller meals, especially when time was of the essence, as it nearly always is at breakfast. They found that they were unable to eat both cereal and a cooked breakfast and so cereal – and toast – won the day. Only at the weekends did a hot meal survive.

When finally doctors, nutritionists and dieticians started to talk about cholesterol levels and heart disease, it emerged that the traditional British breakfast had not been as healthy or as good for you as the previous generations had believed. It was high in saturated animal fats and low in fibre – what was required was a meal that was exactly the reverse.

THE IMPORTANCE OF BREAKFAST

Nutritionists all agree that breakfast is an important – if not *the* most important – meal of the day. Assuming that you sleep for eight hours, and have not eaten for at least two hours before going to bed, your body has been without food for at least ten hours. At this stage it lives on its reserves of carbohydrate and fat – a perfectly normal situation and one that it copes with quite happily.

Should you then on waking just grab a quick cup of instant coffee and rush out of the house without eating anything until lunchtime, you extend the period during which you are living on your reserves for a further four to five hours and this puts the body under stress. The blood sugar level becomes dangerously low with the result that reactions become slower, making you more accident prone and careless as well as more nervous and generally apathetic.

A report published a few years ago found that schoolchildren who did not eat any breakfast were, by mid-morning, far less able to assimilate the information that was being given to them. In some instances, depending on the child's metabolism and general level of intelligence, the later morning lessons were in effect a complete waste of time as concentration was so poor. School timetables for the under-12s now schedule the 3Rs accordingly.

While it may not be as relaxing and enjoyable, nutritionally it is better to eat a good breakfast than it is to eat a large meal in the evening. Eating late at night, when there is only a short time for the food to be digested before going to bed, puts a much greater strain on the digestive system.

Many slimmers find that by eating a sensible breakfast and lunch, without being *too* calorie conscious, and having just a light snack in the evening they can lose weight. This is because the food eaten earlier in the day is quickly burnt off by general exercise. Missing breakfast altogether, or having only a piece of fruit or slice of dry toast, is another reason why diets often fail. In order to stave off the hunger pangs that occur towards the end of the morning, slimmers frequently find it impossible to resist a little nibble—and feeling that they have sinned for the day, think that there is little point in continuing with the diet that day and decide to start again tomorrow!

THE MODERN HEALTHY BREAKFAST

40 g All-Bran
= 11.4 g fibre

50 g muesli
= 7.0 g fibre

50 g porridge
= 3.0 g fibre

50 g wholemeal
toast
= 4.2 g fibre

Research has now proved that diet plays a vitally important part in good health. Firstly it has been established that saturated fats and sugar are harmful to the body, and secondly that for a well-balanced diet one should consume 30 grammes (just over an ounce) of fibre a day.

Sufficient fibre in the diet is thought to eliminate a number of typical Western diseases, including bowel cancer, diverticulitis, appendicitis, gallstones and varicose veins. It is found in a variety of fruit, vegetables, cereals and nuts. Wholemeal flour, for example, contains 2.4 g per oz, raw oatmeal 1.7 g, and peanuts and new potatoes 2.0 g.

Breakfast is an ideal time for consuming some of your fibre quota. A 40 g (just under 2 oz) bowl of All-Bran will provide 11.4 g, i.e. just over a third of the day's requirements. A 50 g bowl of muesli with dried fruit and nuts will give 7.0 g, a similar-sized bowl of porridge 3.0 g, and a 50 g slice of wholemeal toast 4.2 g. Ideally the cereals should be eaten without sugar and be accompanied by skimmed or semi-skimmed milk or natural yoghurt, and the toast should be spread with a low-fat spread or polyunsaturated sunflower margarine and a low-sugar jam or marmalade.

Vitamin C, which is found in fresh fruit and vegetables, is vitally important in helping the body to withstand infections, especially coughs and colds. Precede your high fibre cereal or toast with a glass of freshly squeezed orange juice (this contains some fibre and a lot more Vitamin C than a pre-prepared juice) and you will, according to the experts, be eating the perfect meal to start the day!

YOGHURT WITH WHEATGERM

Served with two or three pieces of fresh fruit, this forms one of the lunches in the Light Diet Room at Grayshott Hall Health Farm. I think that it also makes a very refreshing breakfast.

Homemade yoghurt (which is what they use) is ideal, but failing that use a good-quality low-fat variety. Sprinkle the yoghurt with about 1 tablespoon of wheatgerm before serving. If you like, you can mix the yoghurt with fresh fruit first. Good combinations are sliced banana, kiwi fruit, nectarines and fresh tangerine segments.

BRAN LOAF

If you have never found the prospect of a bowl of All-Bran particularly appealing, this bran loaf is an extremely palatable way of eating it. It keeps well in a tin for at least a week.

4 oz (100 g) All-Bran
5 oz (125 g) light muscovado sugar
10 oz (275 g) mixed dried fruit
½ pint (300 ml) semi-skimmed milk
4 oz (100 g) wholemeal self-raising flour

Put the All-Bran, sugar and dried fruit into a bowl. Stir in the milk, cover and leave to soak overnight. Beat in the flour and mix well. Turn into a greased 1½ lb (675 g) loaf tin and bake in a moderate oven, 350°F/180°C/Gas 4, for 1 hour. Cool in the tin for 5 minutes, then turn out on to a wire rack to cool. Serve, cut in slices.

KHOSHAF

This Middle Eastern fruit salad makes a wonderful breakfast dish, but does require a little forethought as the fruit need to soak for 48 hours. Try to buy the fruit from a health food store, as this way you can be certain that sulphur dioxide has not been used to help dry the fruit, and that they have not been coated with mineral oil to make them shiny and, theoretically, more attractive.

2 oz (50 g) prunes
2 oz (50 g) dried apricots or peaches
2 oz (50 g) dried figs
2 oz (50 g) raisins
2 tablespoons blanched almonds
2 tablespoons chopped walnuts
1 tablespoon rose water

Put the dried fruit into a bowl, cover with cold water and put into the refrigerator for 48 hours. Stir in the nuts and rose water and serve, either on its own or topped with a spoonful of yoghurt.

Serves 4

THE BREAKFAST KINGS

WILLIAM KEITH KELLOGG
(1860–1951)

When William Keith Kellogg and his brother Dr John Harvey Kellogg developed a new health food for Dr John's sanitorium in Battle Creek, Michigan, they had no idea that their work was going to change the breakfast habits of half the Western World.

In 1876, John Kellogg graduated from Bellevue Hospital Medical School and returned to his native town of Battle Creek to take over the Seventh Day Adventist sanitorium. The aims of the clinic stressed '. . . the principle of healing through Nature's simple restorative methods; water treatments, proper rest, exercise, correct mental hygiene and simple food. Restoration of health without the use of drugs was the goal. The diet excluded tea, coffee, meats, condiments, highly seasoned foods and alcoholic drinks.' The clinic drew its patients from all over the United States.

A variety of health foods were made for use in the sanitorium and, as its fame increased, many of the patients wished to continue the regime after they had returned home. This resulted in the Sanitas Food Company being set up to market the products by mail order. It was in their attempt to produce a more digestible, but still palatable, substitute for bread that the brothers managed after considerable difficulty to make a wheat flake. This was produced by first boiling the wheat, leaving it to soak or 'temper', then crushing it between rollers, and finally baking it in the oven. They called it Granose and it quickly found favour with the sanitorium patients and the mail order customers.

No one is certain exactly when the first *corn* flake was produced, but it was in either 1897 or 1898. The early flakes were not a great success as the brothers tried to follow the same formula they'd used for Granose, i.e. using whole corn. Further experimentation found that superior flakes could be obtained by using corn grits or pieces, and that the flavour was improved if malt was added as well. Its popularity increased.

By 1903 Will had started writing in red ink on a number of Sanitas product the words 'Beware of imitations. None genuine without this signature, W.K. Kellogg.' The brothers had experienced severe financial losses with other companies entering the health food market with competitive products. Between 1902 and 1904 no fewer than 42 companies had set up in Battle Creek to market cereals.

In 1906, spurred on by a new marketing adviser, Will decided that for cornflakes he would drop the Sanitas name and call them simply Kellogg's Cornflakes. And so one of the biggest food companies in the world was formed.

A heavy advertising campaign for cornflakes in 1907 quickly achieved results. They became so popular that at one time the factory was unable to keep up with demand and had to beg the housewives of Chicago to stop buying them for 30 days – a certain way to ensure that people would want them even more!

Gradually a rift developed between the two brothers. Will, who had initially been the accountant and administrator at the sanitorium, and was very much in the shadow of his illustrious brother, realised the great potential of flaked cereals, especially corn, if it was properly marketed. John, as a doctor, saw them purely as a health food which should not be openly advertised. Their disagreement was further heightened when Will decided that the company name should be changed from Sanitas to W.K. Kellogg, and that sugar should be added to the flakes. Among other factors, this led to a lengthy lawsuit in 1916, which was eventually won by W.K.

By the start of the 1920s flaked cereals had become an American institution, and in 1922 the first supplies of cornflakes and All-Bran arrived in Britain via Canada. The success of these easily prepared breakfast cereals was immediate and in 1938 Kellogg's opened their first factory in Manchester.

DR MAX BIRCHER-BENNER
(1867–1939)

At the same time that Dr Kellogg was trying to cure his patients by diet in the USA, in Switzerland Dr Max Bircher-Benner was proclaiming that good nutrition was the key to Healthy Living. Like Dr Kellogg, he banned the use of alcohol, tea and coffee at his clinic in Zurich and further insisted that all his patients ate their food raw.

His inspiration for eating raw food originated when he had an attack of jaundice and felt unable to eat anything. At the time it was considered quite dangerous to eat any kind of food raw – even fruit – but his wife gave him a piece of raw apple to eat and almost immediately he felt considerably better. Not long after this he had a patient who was dying as she seemed quite unable to digest her food. A colleague suggested to him that he try an ancient cure of Pythagoras from 500 BC, which was to treat people with digestive difficulties with honey, goat's milk and mashed raw fruit. With some scepticism – literally a case of kill or cure – he tried it, and it worked. This amazing recovery set him off on a lifetime's work of research into the value of raw food.

At the turn of the century he founded his now celebrated clinic, which still stands on the same site 80 years later and which he called *Sanitorium Lebendige Kraft* (Sanatorium of Active Power). Like many pioneers he was ridiculed for his beliefs, in particular by the medical profession. But some of the cures he achieved were really quite remarkable. He was convinced, as indeed many people are now, that you should not just treat the symptoms of the disease, but the body as a whole.

After all the research, care and devotion he invested in his Clinic and in his ideas on raw food and healing, he would probably be rather saddened to learn that nearly 50 years after his death he is best known as the creator of muesli. Doubtless though, he would be cheered and delighted by the role it has played in current healthy eating trends.

Bircher-Benner did not actually invent or create muesli. Made by soaking oatmeal in water overnight to soften it, and then adding milk or yoghurt and fruit, muesli has been a popular Swiss peasant dish for centuries. What he did discover was that it was a dish which he could easily adapt to fit in with his raw food programme. This immediately found favour with his patients, and with the clinic's cosmopolitan clientèle muesli's fame spread. For many people it still remains 'Bircher's Muesli'.

Commercially-prepared mueslis do not need soaking overnight, but if you wish to try the original version this is the authentic recipe:

THE RAW FRUIT PORRIDGE

2 or 3 small *apples* or one large one (7 oz). Clean them by rubbing with a dry cloth. Do not take away the skin, core or pips.

1 level tablespoon *rolled oats* (⅓ oz) previously soaked in 3 tablespoonfuls of water for 12 hours

The juice of half a *lemon*

1 tablespoon sweet *condensed milk* or yoghurt and honey

Nuts: walnuts, hazelnuts, almonds – one tablespoonful grated

First mix condensed milk and lemon juice with soaked rolled oats. Then grate the apples including the skin, core and pips vigorously into the mixture on a two-way grater ('Bircher-Raffel') and whilst doing so, stir frequently. In this way the apple pulp is covered by the mixture and thus prevented from getting brown on contact with the air. It looks white and appetizing. The dish should be prepared immediately before being put on the table. The grated nuts or almonds (1 tablespoonful) which are sprinkled over the dish increase the protein and fat content.

Other fruits suitable for Raw Fruit Porridge: all kinds of soft fruits, plums, apricots, peaches, cherries, strawberries.

P. M. Bircher-Benner

Dr Max Bircher-Benner's recipe for muesli.

FACTS AND FIGURES

Eating a cooked breakfast may no longer be fashionable at home, but as soon as people start travelling and staying away overnight, they start eating it again.

* In 1986, 500,000 Great British Breakfasts were served on Inter-City trains and 130,000 light breakfasts.

* During the course of a day, The Savoy Hotel in London gets through between 200 and 250 *dozen* eggs – though what proportion are breakfast eggs they are not quite certain. They do know, however, that breakfast accounts for 30 lb (13.5 kg) bacon, 5 lb (2.25 kg) kippers and 35–40 loaves of bread.

* Almost seven out of ten people start the day with toast, plain bread, or even sandwiches. White toast tops the popularity poll for breakfast, almost a quarter of the population tucking into white toast first thing. A further 16% choose wholemeal toast and only 6% go for ordinary brown.

* Only 1% have croissants for breakfast, the same number that eat fried bread.

* 4 billion bowls of cereal are consumed in the UK each year, and in any week two out of three people eat a bowl of Kellogg's cereal.

CONTINENTAL BREAKFASTS

FRANCE

As soon as a 'Continental breakfast' is mentioned, people immediately think of rolls, croissants and brioches, served with unsalted butter, apricot jam and coffee. This, however, is merely a French breakfast and other parts of Europe eat breakfasts which are very different. The French have always clung to their large lunches. Breakfast – *le petit déjeuner* (little lunch) or *déjeuner a tasse* (lunch in a cup) – is merely a light meal eaten in order to sustain them through the morning before the real eating begins at lunchtime.

GERMANY AND AUSTRIA

In Germany and Austria they used to eat two breakfasts. The first *fruhstuck* was eaten at home at about 6.30 a.m. before leaving for work. It consisted of fresh bread rolls, rye bread, butter, jam and coffee, although boiled eggs were sometimes eaten as well, particularly in the north of Germany.

The second, *zweites fruhstück*, took place between 9 and 10 o'clock. People working in factories and offices would take this second breakfast to work with them in the form of hearty cheese and sausage (*wurst*) rolls. Simple meals, such as a plate of *wurst* or some goulash, could (and still can) be bought in restaurants, and in Baden in Southern Germany the classic dish for *zweites fruhstück* is rye bread with smoked raw bacon washed down with cherry brandy.

At one time – not that long ago – *zweites fruhstück* was a major social occasion for wealthy men, who would sit in elegant restaurants eating smoked salmon, pâté de foie gras, oysters and caviare, accompanied by plenty of good wine. They felt it necessary to follow Bismarck's advice that, 'If a German wants to be properly conscious of his strength he must first have a half-bottle of wine inside him – or better still a whole bottle.' But in the same way that his British and American counterparts have for the most part abandoned their cooked breakfast, the average German has reduced his breakfasts to just one. In the country areas, however, traditions still hold.

HOLLAND

In neighbouring Holland, breakfast consists of an extensive range of freshly baked breads and rolls, which are served with thin slices of cheese, jam, chocolate vermicelli or sugared, coloured caraway seeds called *muisjes*.

SCANDINAVIA

Cheese is a feature of breakfast in all the Scandinavian countries, where there is always a selection of breads, including rye bread and possibly a fruit bread as well. Danish pastries may appear on the breakfast menu at The Savoy in London and in the States but they are rarely seen on breakfast tables in their native country. That other renowned Danish speciality – the Open Sandwich – is always present, especially for brunch.

SOUTHERN EUROPE

In the south of Europe, bread and rolls served with honey dominate. Yoghurt is popular in Greece and Yugoslavia. In Spain, *churros* are eaten, dunked into the breakfast tea or chocolate. A speciality of Northern Spain are the light, yeast-based pastries called *ensaimadas*.

INTERNATIONAL BREAKFASTS

Hardly surprisingly, rice is the chief ingredient of breakfast in India, China and Japan. The Indians breakfast on little rice cakes, which are generally made at dawn by the woman of the house while the men sleep. Even if she has servants, by tradition she has to do the actual mixing and cooking herself.

The Chinese start their day with a dish of rice fish porridge. A similar sticky rice and fish dish is also served in Japan, together with Egg Tofu. But the essential part of every Japanese breakfast is a Miso Soup – soups made with stock and thickened with bean paste or curd, to which other ingredients such as fish, vegetables, etc. are added.

In tropical countries where the air hangs heavy with the scent of mangoes, pawpaws, passion fruit, mangosteens and bananas, fruit is the mainstay of breakfast. Pawpaw (or papaya if you prefer) features on breakfast menus in every country in which it is grown, from the West Indies and Latin America to East Africa and Indonesia. It is with paw paw (even if accompanied by the more British bacon and eggs) that so many of the characters in Somerset Maugham's short stories start the day.

There are two kinds of pawpaw: the small oval variety with one rather bulbous end, the sort most frequently seen in the UK, and larger ones the size of a melon. If you are eating pawpaw *au naturel*, squeeze a little lime or lemon juice on to the flesh to bring out its full flavour.

BREAKFAST DOWN UNDER

A large rump steak topped with fried egg(s) is considered to be the true Australian breakfast. But with the Australians becoming as health-conscious as the rest of us, this no longer holds true, and certainly in the cities you are far more likely to be offered muesli and orange juice.

In the outback, though, they still like a bit of good 'tucker' for their breakfast. On the sheep stations, lambs' fry – a mixture of offal including the brains, kidneys, liver and heart is very popular, especially when made from sheep that have been slaughtered the evening before. The pieces of fresh offal are either quickly dipped in flour and fried, or coated with a light, crisp batter.

BREAKFAST IN THE USA

According to Mark Twain in *A Tramp Abroad* (1879), 'The average American's simplest and commonest form of breakfast consists of coffee and beefsteak.' At the turn of the century, breakfast in the USA was almost as great a feast as it was in Britain, but with slight differences in the foods consumed. A typical breakfast was steak and potatoes, a stack of griddle cakes or waffles with syrup, two eggs with ham and bacon, and a wedge of apple pie.

Both waffles and griddle cakes are old English dishes. Waffles used to be served at banquets in Medieval England, but their popularity in the States has more to do with the later German and Dutch settlers than with the Pilgrim Fathers.

Like all American food, their breakfast dishes are a wonderful hotch-potch of cuisines. Bagels and cream cheese are immensely popular in New York and come from the cuisines of Jewish immigrants and other Middle Europeans. Blinis have similar origins, whereas Virginia Spoon Bread has a distinctive French feel to it.

While breakfast today in health-conscious California consists only of fresh fruit juice (from organically grown fruit), muesli and herb tea, in other parts of the States it is an institution that still survives.

HASH BROWNS

The traditional American accompaniment to bacon and eggs. Ideally the potatoes should be fried in bacon fat to give them plenty of flavour, and in some recipes strips of crispy bacon are added.

Americans are far more fussy than we are about the way their fried eggs are served: they refer to them as 'over-easy' or 'over-light' when the eggs are turned during cooking so that the thin film of white over the yolk becomes cooked, or 'sunny-side up' when it is not.

2 lb (900 g) potatoes
2 oz (50 g) bacon fat or beef dripping
freshly milled black pepper

Peel the potatoes, cut them into ½ inch (1.25 cm) cubes and cook in boiling salted water for 8 minutes. Drain thoroughly. Heat the bacon fat in a large frying pan. Add the potatoes, then press them down with a fish slice or spatula so that they form a cake. Grind over some black pepper. Cook for a further 8 minutes or until the potatoes on the underside are crisp and golden brown. Remove from the heat, cover with a plate and leave to steam for 2 minutes.

Invert the hash browns on to the plate, then slide back into the pan and cook for a further 5 minutes, or until the underside is golden brown. Slide or invert on to a serving plate.

Serves 4–6

APPLE AND RAISIN MUFFINS

American muffins are completely different from English muffins; the latter being made from a yeast dough, while the former are raised with baking powder. The early settlers had a shortage of fresh yeast, hence their production of other non-yeasted breads such as sourdough. Muffins are standard American breakfast fare, either plain, made with bran or, as in this recipe, with fruit added to them.

7 oz (200 g) plain flour
1 tablespoon baking powder
1/2 teaspoon salt
2 oz (50 g) caster sugar
1 cooking apple, peeled, cored and finely chopped
2 oz (50 g) raisins
8 fl oz (200 ml) milk
1 egg, beaten
2 oz (50 g) melted butter

Well butter 12-15 deep patty tins. Mix the flour, baking powder, salt and sugar in a bowl. Add the apple and raisins. Mix the milk with the beaten egg and stir in the butter. Add to the dry ingredients and stir lightly, just enough to mix the ingredients. Spoon into the prepared tins, filling them just over half full.

Bake in a moderately hot oven, 400°F/200°C/ Gas 6 for 15–20 minutes or until well risen and golden brown. Remove from the tins and serve hot.

BREAKFAST MEETINGS

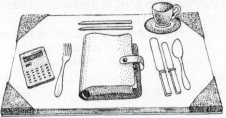

David Frost is reputed to be the man who brought the idea of breakfast meetings across the Atlantic. Part of the everyday life of the American executive, fashionable hotels are cashing in on the business breakfast and the dining room suites of large industrial companies, manufacturers and advertising agencies are starting to buzz with activity from 7.30 a.m. onwards as major decisions are made over delectable Cumberland sausages, Arbroath smokies or trout fishcakes.

In London, The Connaught, The Ritz and The Savoy serve some of the best food with the widest choice, but a number of American fast food chains, accustomed to serving brunch, are now increasing the options.

A practical move for today's society, it is not one of which Oscar Wilde would have approved, having observed that 'Only dull people are brilliant at breakfast.' But it does perhaps solve A.P. Herbert's problem, that 'the critical period in matrimony is breakfast time.'

TROUT FISHCAKES

These fishcakes bear no resemblance to the rather dry, tasteless objects sold in most frozen food stores. A mixture of fresh and smoked trout, coated in fresh white breadcrumbs, they are at their best served with grilled bacon and accompanied by Sauce Robert – a slightly spicy tomato ketchup which can be found in many good grocers and delicatessens.

8 oz (225 g) cooked trout (weight without skin and bone)
4 oz (100 g) smoked trout (weight without skin and bone)
8 oz (225 g) cooked potatoes
1 egg yolk
1 tablespoon chopped parsley
1 teaspoon anchovy essence
1 tablespoon lemon juice
salt and freshly milled black pepper

For coating
1 egg white
1 whole egg
a little seasoned flour
3 oz (75 g) fresh white breadcrumbs
oil and butter for frying

Flake the flesh of the fresh and smoked trout and mash lightly in a basin. Sieve in the potatoes, then add the remaining ingredients and mix together. Season well with salt and pepper.

Lightly flour your hands and form the mixture into six round cakes about 3 inches (7.5 cm) in diameter. If you have time, put them into the refrigerator for 30 minutes as this makes the mixture stiffer and easier to coat.

Beat the egg white with the egg yolk on a plate. Sprinkle some seasoned flour on another plate, and tip the breadcrumbs on to a third. Dip the fish cakes first in the flour, then in the egg and finally toss in the breadcrumbs.

When all the fishcakes have been coated fry them in a mixture of butter and oil until they are crisp and golden brown. Serve hot.

Serves 6

SALMON FISHCAKES

For salmon fishcakes, use 12 oz (375 g) cooked salmon and proceed as above.

FISHCAKES WITH CAPERS

Make either trout or salmon fishcakes as above and add 1 tablespoon chopped capers.

BRUNCH

Brunch is generally thought of as an all-American institution, but at the turn of the century it was a popular meal amongst a number of Oxford's less academic undergraduates. Wining, dining and revelling into the early hours of the morning, they rose late and found it simpler to join breakfast and lunch into one meal.

> 'Hardened night-birds fondly cherish,
> All the subtle charms of brunch'.
> *Westminster Gazette*, 1900

Despite these early attempts at making brunch a British way of life, it has never been as popular here as it is in the USA. In New York there are countless restaurants serving brunch from 9 or 10 a.m. through to the middle of the afternoon any day of the week.

Weekends and public holidays are the times when brunch really comes into its own, whichever side of the Atlantic you are on. This is the only opportunity most people have to enjoy this meal, which should be eaten leisurely, in the same way that the Victorians and Edwardians consumed their vast breakfasts. Those same foods are ideal for brunch, and as brunch parties frequently take the form of buffets people even wander round collecting their food themselves as they would have done 100 years ago.

CRUSTY HADDOCK BAKE

Haddock, corn and bacon team up well together and make a perfect brunch dish. Prepare in advance.

1½ lb (675 g) smoked haddock fillets
1 pint (600 ml) milk and black pepper
1 oz (25 g) butter
8 oz (225 g) smoked streaky bacon, de-rinded, chopped
1½ oz (40 g) flour
¼ pint (150 ml) single cream
7 oz (195 g) can sweetcorn kernels, drained
4 slices buttered wholemeal bread

Place the smoked haddock in a pan with the milk and a good grinding of black pepper. Cover and poach gently for about 5 minutes, then remove from the heat and allow to cool. Drain the fish, reserving the milk. Skin and flake the flesh.

Heat the butter in a pan, add the bacon and cook gently for about 10 minutes or until much of the fat has run out of the bacon. Remove the bacon from the pan with a draining spoon and add to the haddock. Stir the flour into the fat and cook for a minute, then gradually stir in the fish liquor and bring to the boil, stirring all the time. Stir in the cream, haddock and bacon, and the corn. Taste and adjust the seasoning. Turn into an ovenproof dish.

Cut the bread into triangles and arrange on top of the fish mixture. Bake in a moderately hot oven, 400°F/200°C/Gas 6 for 30 minutes. Serve hot.

Serves 8

BLINIS

The New Yorker's ideal brunch – blinis made with buckwheat flour, topped with soured cream and lumpfish roe. The yeasted mixture should be made the night before and then left to rise in the refrigerator overnight.

1 teaspoon caster sugar
¾ pint (450 ml) warm milk
3 teaspoons dried yeast
6 oz (175 g) buckwheat flour
6 oz (175 g) plain flour
1 teaspoon salt
1½ oz (45 g) butter, melted
3 eggs separated

For frying
approx 2 oz (50 g) butter, melted

For the topping
½ pint (300 ml) soured cream
4 oz (100 g) caviare style lumpfish roe

Dissolve the sugar in the warm milk, sprinkle over the yeast and leave for 10 minutes or until frothy. Sift the flours and salt into a bowl. Pour over the yeast mixture, beat well, then cover and leave in the refrigerator overnight, or for about 12 hours. Remove from the refrigerator and allow to come to room temperature for about 30 minutes.

Beat in the melted butter, then the egg yolks.

Whisk the egg whites until they are just stiff, then fold into the mixture. Leave at room temperature for 30 minutes.

Heat a griddle or thick frying pan, add a little butter, then pour in about 2 tablespoons of the batter, allowing it to spread out. When the top is set and full of bubbles, lightly brush with more butter, turn and cook on the second side, until golden brown. You should be able to cook about 3 blinis at a time, depending on the size of the frying pan or griddle. When cooked, remove from the pan and keep warm while frying the remainder.

Pile the blinis on to a serving plate and serve the soured cream and lumpfish roe in separate bowls. Guests should help themselves, first spreading a spoonful of soured cream on the pancake and topping this with a teaspoon of lumpfish roe.

Serves 8

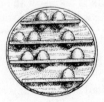

THE CAFFEINE RELATIONSHIP

The majority of people in Europe and the USA start their day with a cup of tea or a cup of coffee. Some may drink chocolate. All three beverages contain the stimulant caffeine, although the quantity in chocolate is lower, the principle stimulant there being theobromine.

The effect of caffeine is to stimulate the central nervous system, so that the heart rate is slightly increased and the blood vessels dilate. This effect is obviously heightened when, as at breakfast or on waking, the drink is taken on an empty stomach. It is difficult to be exact about how much caffeine there is in a cup of tea or coffee; the amount is influenced by a number of factors, such as the type of coffee bean or tea leaf, how it was roasted or dried, etc. As a guide, an average cup of coffee contains about 100 milligrams, a small cup of strong expresso can have as much as 200, but a cup of tea has only 70. Theobromine works in a slightly different way, which is why some people find chocolate gives them a similar 'lift' without any of the possible side effects of caffeine.

Taken in moderation, caffeine is generally considered to be harmless and many people find they need that little 'kick' to get them going in the morning. Its benefits were described by Dr J. Murdoch Ritchie who, in the 1970 edition of *The Pharmacological Basis of Therapeutics*, concluded that 'After taking caffeine one is capable of greater sustained intellectual effort and a more perfect association of ideas. There is also a keener appreciation of sensory stimuli and . . . motor activity is increased; typists, for example, work faster and with fewer errors.'

BREAKFAST TEAS AND COFFEES

The British have always taken their tea-drinking seriously, with the result that – unlike the Europeans who hardly touch the stuff – there is a vast range of breakfast teas and afternoon teas available.

Most people like a fairly strong, robust tea for breakfast, such as an Assam, Darjeeling or a Ceylon, or a special breakfast blend. When it comes to coffee it is the exact opposite: the dark, rich roasts being reserved for after dinner, and the lighter ones for breakfast. Of the pure, unblended beans, the South American ones are generally the most popular for breakfast, including Columbian, Costa Rican and Nicaraguan.

CHAMPAGNE BREAKFASTS

Like brunches, champagne breakfasts and breakfast parties are enjoying a resurgence of popularity, but these days tend to be weekend and especially Sunday affairs.

Buck's Fizz – that great innovation of Buck's Club, consisting of chilled fresh orange juice and champagne – is more frequently consumed at an early hour than straight champagne. Unlike our ancestors, who quaffed ale on rising, most of us are not quite up to straight alcohol as we hop out of bed! Buck's Fizz also has the advantage that you can get away with using a sparkling white wine rather than the real McCoy! The usual bacon, egg, sausages, mushrooms, etc. can all be served on these occasions, but to accompany the champagne there is little to beat Scrambled Eggs with Smoked Salmon.

SCRAMBLED EGGS WITH SMOKED SALMON

There are two ways of preparing this delicious dish. You can either lay thin slices of smoked salmon on individual plates, and then spoon the hot scrambled egg into the centre, or you can add thin strips of smoked salmon to the egg when it is cooked, allowing 1 oz (25 g) smoked salmon to every two eggs. Whichever method you choose, the most important thing is to have Perfect Scrambled Eggs.

PER PERSON
2 eggs
salt and freshly milled black pepper
1/2 oz (15 g) butter
2 tablepoons double (or single) cream

Beat the eggs and season with salt and freshly milled black pepper. Melt the butter in a pan over a gentle heat. Pour in the eggs and cook, stirring frequently until the eggs are *just* set. *Immediately* remove from the heat and briskly stir in 1 tablespoon of cream per egg, preferably double cream though single can be used. The coldness of the cream immediately arrests the cooking process, so you don't have the problem of the egg continuing to cook in the pan after it has been removed from the heat.

Serve as soon as possible after cooking, but if you need to keep the scrambled eggs warm for a short while, put them in a bowl and stand it in a dish of hot water.

BREAKFAST FAVOURITES

MARMALADE

No matter what kind of breakfast is served, as soon as toast is mentioned, it has to be accompanied by marmalade. There are various stories about the origin of the word 'marmalade', all of which feature Mary, Queen of Scots, who had developed a passion for this preserve while in exile in France.

One theory is that the word is a corruption of '*Marie-malade*', as whenever Mary was sick she would request some of her favourite preserve. Another has it that marmalade was first made for her by her Spanish doctor as a cure for sea-sickness, so was given the name '*mer-malade*'. What is in fact far more likely is that the word is a corruption either of *marmelo*, the Spanish for quince, or a stiff paste-like preserve made from quinces in Portugal called *mermelada*.

Although not produced commercially until the late 18th century, a form of the preserve, possibly made with sweet oranges, was produced in Scottish homes from the time of their troubled Queen Mary.

The start of commercial production in Scotland is a tale of proverbial Scottish thrift. A Spanish ship laden with Seville oranges took refuge in Dundee harbour. Thinking he had made a great bargain, a local man, James Keiller, purchased the cargo at a rock bottom price, only to find that the oranges were far too bitter to eat and that he was unable to sell them. His wife, Janet, worried that her husband was about to incur a major loss, decided that the only thing to do was to make them into marmalade. The end result was such a success and proved so popular that she repeated the experiment, and in the year 1797 the firm of James Keiller and Son was established.

Nearly a century later other Scots went into marmalade production Margaret Baxter in Speyside, and the Robertsons in Paisley. It was the Robertsons who first produced the renowned 'Golden Shred' marmalade. South of the border in Oxford in 1874, the wife of a grocer called Frank Cooper began making a 'vintage marmalade' from an old family recipe, which immediately became highly prized by both the dons and undergraduates alike.

Nowadays other citrus fruit such as lemons, limes, grapefruit and sweet oranges are also used to make marmalade. Whilst most commercially-produced marmalade is excellent, many people feel that you cannot better a good home-made chunky variety, such as the one that follows.

CHUNKY SEVILLE MARMALADE

The addition of 2 tablespoons of black treacle gives a rich, dark colour and flavour to this marmalade.

3 lb (1.2 kilo) Seville oranges
3 lemons
6 pints (3.5 litres) water
6 lb (2.4 kilo) preserving or granulated sugar
2 tablespoons black treacle or molasses

Wash the fruit and put into a large saucepan with water, cover with a lid or foil and bring to the boil. Simmer the fruit for 1½ hours, turning and stirring it three or four times.

Remove from the heat. When cool enough to handle remove the fruit and cut each piece in half. Scoop out all the pulp with a dessertspoon and put this into the cooking juices in the pan, together with the pips (reserve the peel). Bring to the boil and boil rapidly for 15 minutes, then strain through a sieve into the preserving pan. Leave the pulp to drain for about 15 minutes to extract all the juice.

Meanwhile, cut the peel into shreds and add to the juices in the pan. Stir in the sugar and treacle, stir over a moderate heat until the sugar has dissolved, then bring to the boil, stirring from time to time.

Boil rapidly to 105°F/220°C until setting point is reached. Allow to cool for about 10 minutes, then pour into heated jars, cover and seal.

Makes about 10 lb (4.5 kg)

PORRIDGE

Traditionally porridge was always eaten (certainly by the men) while standing up and walking round the room. Various reasons are given for this, the best known one being that if you ate your porridge standing up with your back to the wall, your enemy would not be able to creep up from behind and stab you in the back while you were eating it! A wise precaution in the days of the murdering clans. It has also been suggested that it was because 'A stanin' sack fills fu'est', and when one considers that for many people their morning porridge was all they had to sustain them through a full and hard day's labour until the evening meal, it made good sense to eat plenty of it.

For many hundreds of years porridge was Scotland's staple food. In 1703 M. Martin, Gent., wrote in his *Description of the Western Isles* that 'oatmeal, boiled with water, with some bread, is the constant food of both sexes in this and other islands during winter and spring, yet they go under many fatigues by sea and land, and are very healthful.' It may no longer occupy a role of anything like that importance, but the ritual of making, serving and eating porridge is still a subject close to the heart of most Scots.

A true Scot would be horrified at the idea of making porridge with milk, a practice frequently carried out south of the border. As for eating it with sugar, honey or syrup, considered by most Southerners to be an integral part of the dish, that is almost sacrilegious – for them porridge should only be flavoured with salt.

MAKING PORRIDGE

Porridge oats are considered to be *almost* acceptable, but for the purist only medium oatmeal, preferably from Midlothian, and fresh spring water will do.

For two people, you need 2 heaped tablespoons of oatmeal and 2 cups of water. The water should be brought to the boil in a large pan and the oatmeal poured in a thin steady stream with the left hand. At the same time, the mixture should be stirred with the right hand in a clockwise direction, using a porridge stick, known variously as a 'theevil', 'spurtle' or 'gruel-tree'. These sticks are still produced (albeit mainly for the tourist trade with a thistle carved into the end!), but previously they were considered an essential part of porridge making and one of the first items acquired for a young woman's bottom drawer.

Once the mixture has thickened it should be simmered for about 20 minutes, stirring frequently to prevent it from burning and sticking to the base of the pan. Shortly before serving, salt should be added to taste (this should not be added before the oatmeal is fully cooked or it will harden it).

The porridge should be ladled into bowls or porringers and eaten with a hornspoon – because if the porridge is piping hot a metal spoon will become too hot to hold! The correct way to eat porridge is to have a separate bowl of milk, cream or buttermilk, and to dip every spoonful of porridge into the milk, etc., to cool in it before eating. In practice though, most people simply pour milk, etc, over the porridge in the bowl.

'The halesome parritch,
Chief of 'Scotia's food'

Robert Burns (1759-96)

KIPPERS

'I don't know if you have ever noticed it, Jeeves, but a good spirited kipper first thing in the morning seems to put heart into you'.

P.G. Wodehouse *The Mating Season*, 1949

The ban on herring fishing in the 1970s, coupled with 'improved food technology which enabled the fish to be injected and dyed to give a "kipper flavour" ', caused the popularity of the kipper to go into a marked decline. This is tragic as there is nothing to beat the flavour of a true kipper from Lochfyneside in Scotland, or from Great Yarmouth or the Isle of Man. But with the dyes now being removed and a greater awareness of what *good* food should really taste like, properly smoked kippers are starting to make a comeback.

There are various views on how a kipper should be cooked.

* Jugging, the common English method when the kippers were folded in half, put into a jug of boiling water and left for 5 minutes, is now frowned upon.
* Lightly dotting with butter and grilling enables the outside of the flesh to become slightly crisp, while the inside remains moist.
* If you are cooking a pair, a good Scottish method is to place them together with the skin outside and then grill or fry them, turning them once.
* Finally there is the microwave, which is not only quick but cooks all fish to perfection.

SAUSAGES

Sadly many sausages sold today fall a long way short of the delicious, juicy sausages enjoyed by our fore-fathers. Today's sausage is usually full of rusks, pre-servatives and somewhat dubious meat. Fortunately there are a few firms who still produce *real* sausages made from fresh pork (the whole pig, not trim-mings), bread and spices, and encase them in natural skins rather than synthetic ones.

One such sausage-maker is Musks of Newmarket, Suffolk, who were established in 1884 and held the Royal Warrant for King George V and Edward VII when he was Prince of Wales. Currently they hold the Royal Warrant for Queen Elizabeth the Queen Mother. Her order is not large, but is religiously despatched each week, although recently she went without. A new delivery driver informed Musks the following week that he had been unable to deliver the sausages to Clarence House as there was no street number on the packet!

There are various schools of thought as to the best way to cook sausages. Arguments centre round whether frying or grilling is preferable. If serving hot, sausages are possibly best fried slowly, without any additional fat, but if serving cold, grilling is gen-erally better so that as much fat as possible comes out. Whichever way you choose, do not on any account prick them before cooking. All this does is allow the juices to come out. Provided the sausages are cooked slowly they should not burst.

HANGOVER CURES

Many people swear that the best way to start the day if you are suffering from the excesses of the night before is to eat a classic British cooked breakfast.

KATERFRUHSTÜCK
In Germany they have a special hangover breakfast – the *Katerfruhstück* – which consists of various kinds of rollmops, well spiced and served with soured cream, horseradish and other sauces, followed by sausages and country hams. All washed down by the hair of whichever dog bit in the first place.

For those whose stomachs feel perhaps a little too delicate to embark on such a robust cure, there are other choices available:

CHINA TEA: Copious quantities of weak China tea are very refreshing and will help to rehydrate the body.

TOMATO JUICE: A glass of cold tomato juice topped with a good dash of Worcestershire sauce frequently does the trick, and if taken with a dash of vodka added it is known to work wonders.

HOT CHOCOLATE: Samuel Pepys was convinced of the efficacy of chocolate. The morning after a night of revelry following the Coronation of Charles II he wrote: 'Waked this morning with my head in a sad taking through last night's drink, which I am very sorry for. So rise and went out with Mr Creed to drink our morning draught, which he did give me in chocolate to settle my stomach.'

This doubtless fortified him for breakfast prepared by Mrs Pepys, who was reputed to be an indifferent cook and usually gave him either eggs or a red herring on his return home.

PRAIRIE OYSTER: This may take a little courage but is said to be the perfect cure. Break a raw egg into a glass, mix lightly with a few drops of Worcestershire sauce and drink – quickly!

OTHER TITLES IN THE SERIES